TABLE OF CONTENTS

INTRODUCTION

Want to see your money really go places? Why not fold those bills into fantastic paper airplanes? In *Paper Airplanes with Dollar Bills*, 13 different paper airplane designs are drawn out step-by-step. And there is no need to go to the store and buy special craft paper—so save that money to use for the planes! None of the projects in this book involve any type of cutting, drawing, taping, or tearing the bill, so no currency defacement laws will be broken. Crisp, new bills will work the best.

New to paper folding? There are basic folds explained in the beginning of the book, folds which are used throughout the projects. Sprinkled between the airplanes are some cool money facts. If you want to learn even more about our greenbacks, visit www.moneyfactory.com, the website of the Bureau of Engraving and Printing.

Practice makes perfect. So save those dollar bills, turn them into super flying planes, and see your money fly!

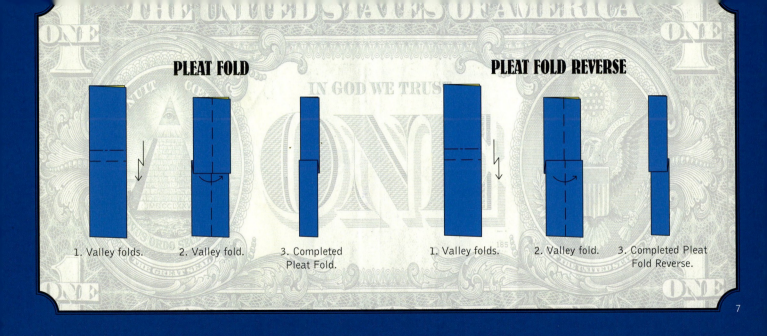

PLEAT FOLD

1. Valley folds.

2. Valley fold.

3. Completed Pleat Fold.

PLEAT FOLD REVERSE

1. Valley folds.

2. Valley fold.

3. Completed Pleat Fold Reverse.

BASE FOLD

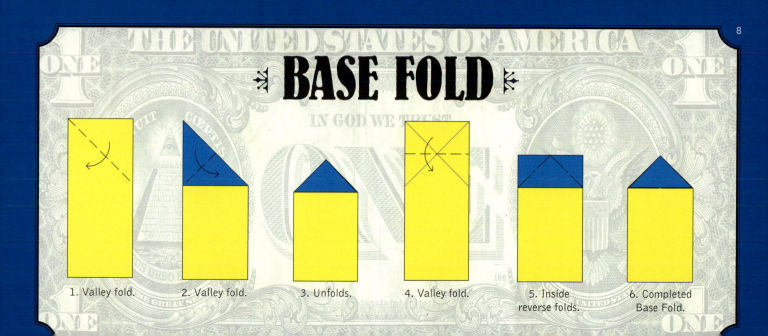

1. Valley fold.

2. Valley fold.

3. Unfolds.

4. Valley fold.

5. Inside reverse folds.

6. Completed Base Fold.

F-14A TOMCAT

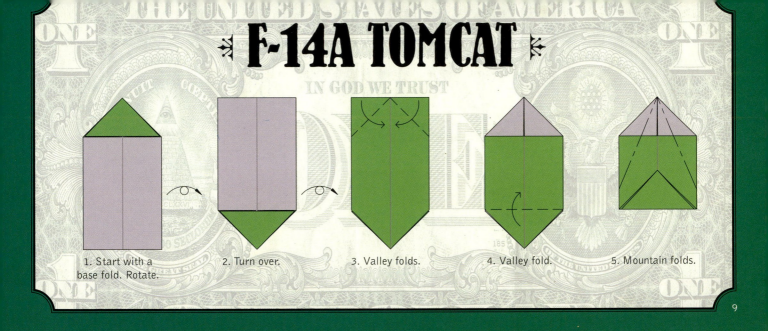

1. Start with a base fold. Rotate.

2. Turn over.

3. Valley folds.

4. Valley fold.

5. Mountain folds.

F-14A TOMCAT

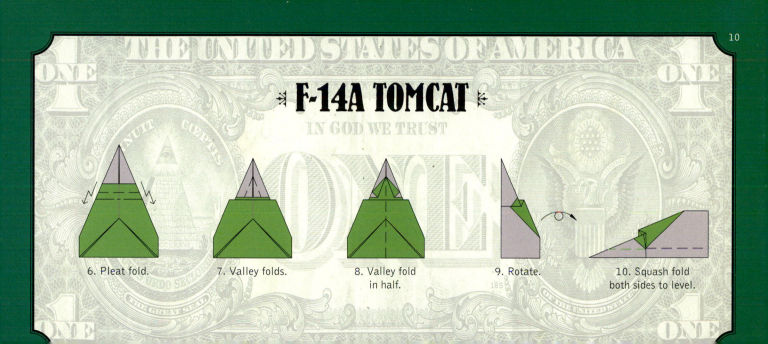

6. Pleat fold.

7. Valley folds.

8. Valley fold in half.

9. Rotate.

10. Squash fold both sides to level.

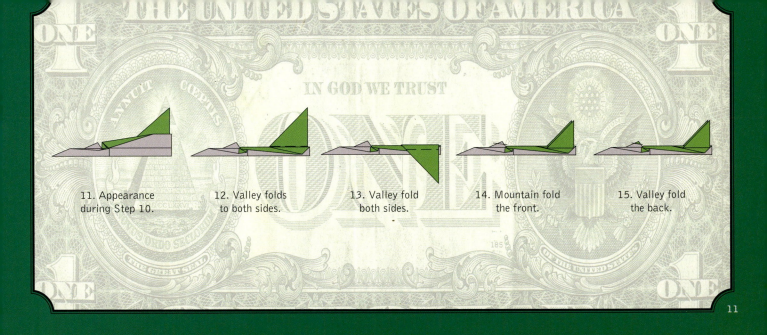

11. Appearance during Step 10.

12. Valley folds to both sides.

13. Valley fold both sides.

14. Mountain fold the front.

15. Valley fold the back.

F-14A TOMCAT

16. Inside
reverse fold.

17. Completed
F-14A Tomcat.

B-2 BOMBER

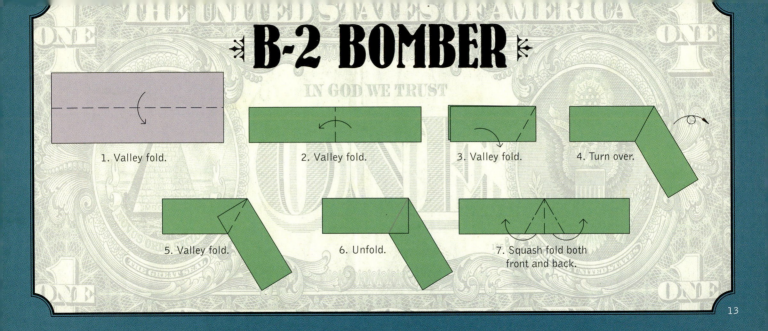

1. Valley fold.

2. Valley fold.

3. Valley fold.

4. Turn over.

5. Valley fold.

6. Unfold.

7. Squash fold both front and back.

B-2 BOMBER

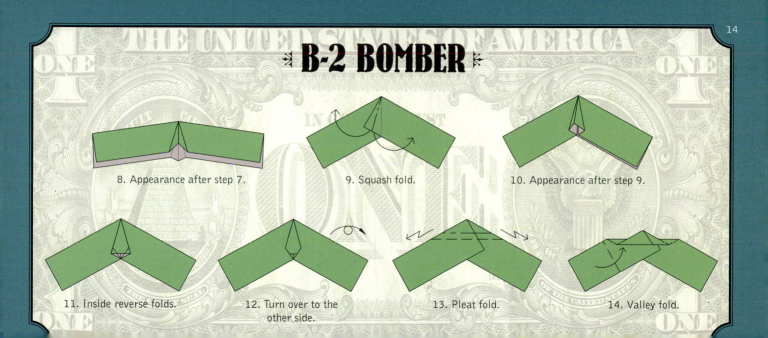

8. Appearance after step 7.

9. Squash fold.

10. Appearance after step 9.

11. Inside reverse folds.

12. Turn over to the other side.

13. Pleat fold.

14. Valley fold.

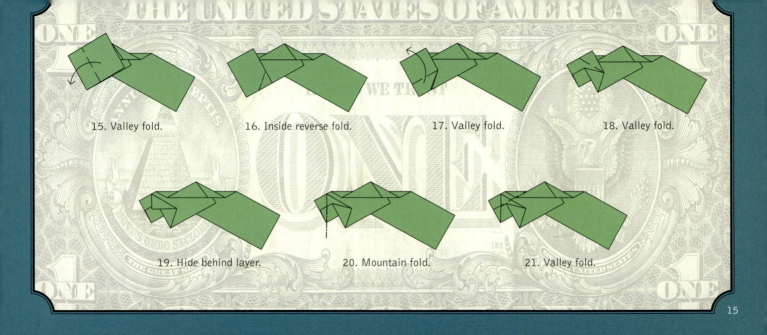

15. Valley fold.

16. Inside reverse fold.

17. Valley fold.

18. Valley fold.

19. Hide behind layer.

20. Mountain fold.

21. Valley fold.

B-2 BOMBER

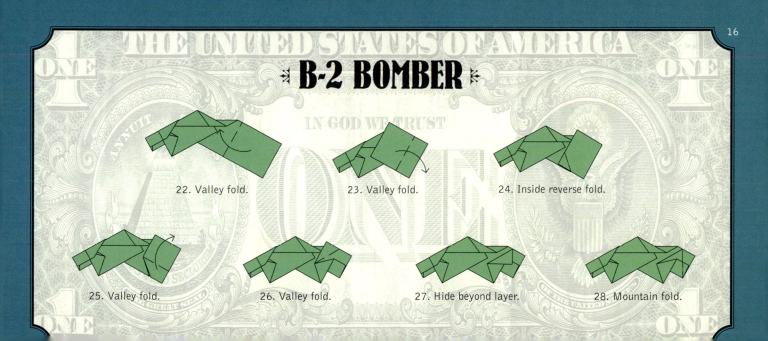

22. Valley fold.

23. Valley fold.

24. Inside reverse fold.

25. Valley fold.

26. Valley fold.

27. Hide beyond layer.

28. Mountain fold.

29. Valley fold.

30. Fold in half.

31. Valley folds.

32. Flatten.

Completed B-2 Bomber,
shown from the top.

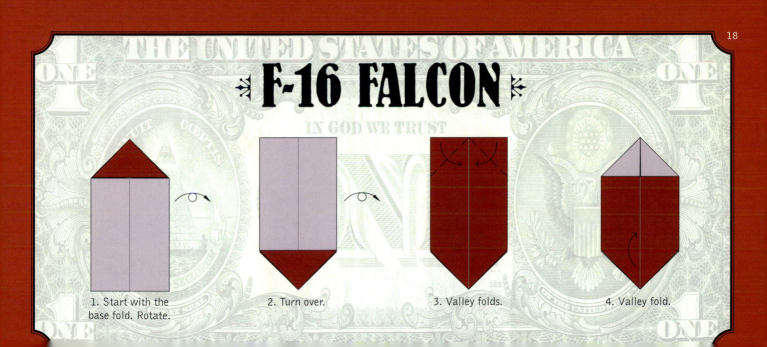

F-16 FALCON

THE UNITED STATES OF AMERICA

IN GOD WE TRUST

1. Start with the base fold. Rotate.

2. Turn over.

3. Valley folds.

4. Valley fold.

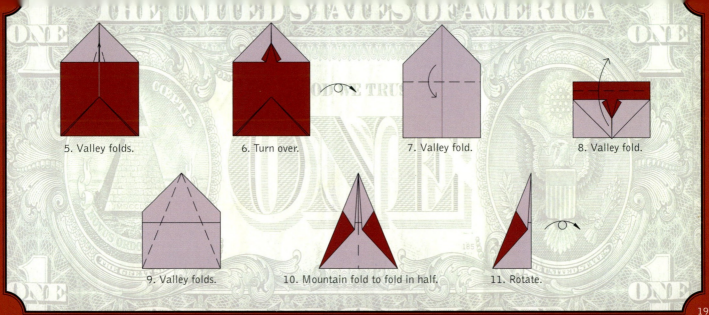

5. Valley folds.

6. Turn over.

7. Valley fold.

8. Valley fold.

9. Valley folds.

10. Mountain fold to fold in half.

11. Rotate.

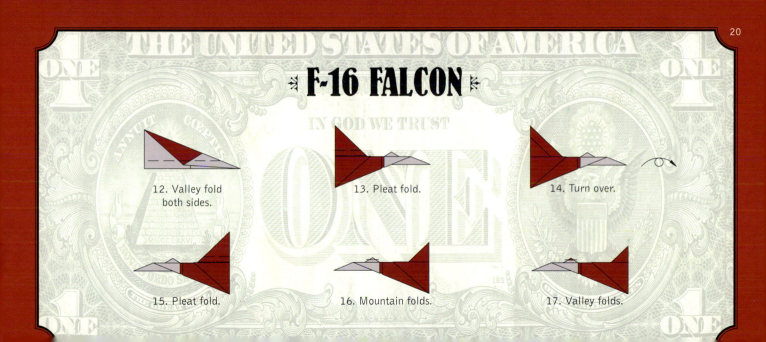

F-16 FALCON

12. Valley fold both sides.

13. Pleat fold.

14. Turn over.

15. Pleat fold.

16. Mountain folds.

17. Valley folds.

18. Valley folds both sides.

19. Level the wings.

Finished F-16 Falcon,
shown from the top.

❊ BATTLE STAR GALACTICA: RAIDER ❊

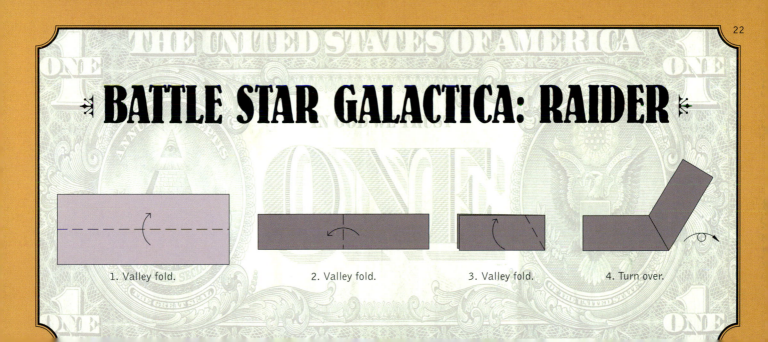

1. Valley fold.

2. Valley fold.

3. Valley fold.

4. Turn over.

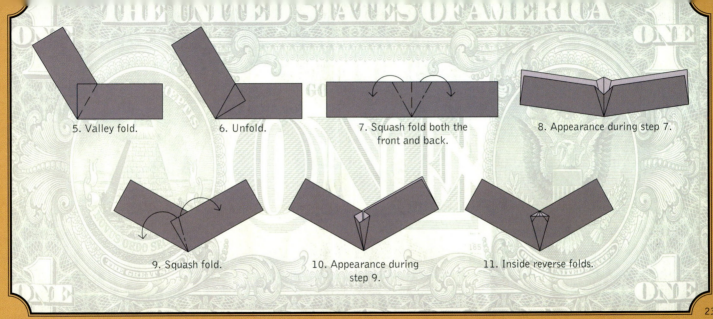

5. Valley fold.

6. Unfold.

7. Squash fold both the front and back.

8. Appearance during step 7.

9. Squash fold.

10. Appearance during step 9.

11. Inside reverse folds.

❋ BATTLE STAR GALACTICA: RAIDER ❋

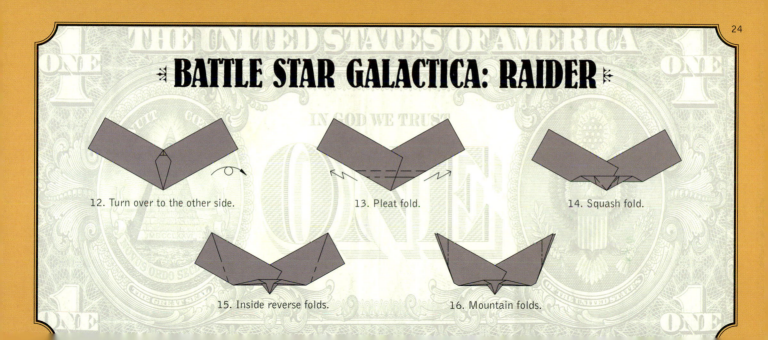

12. Turn over to the other side.

13. Pleat fold.

14. Squash fold.

15. Inside reverse folds.

16. Mountain folds.

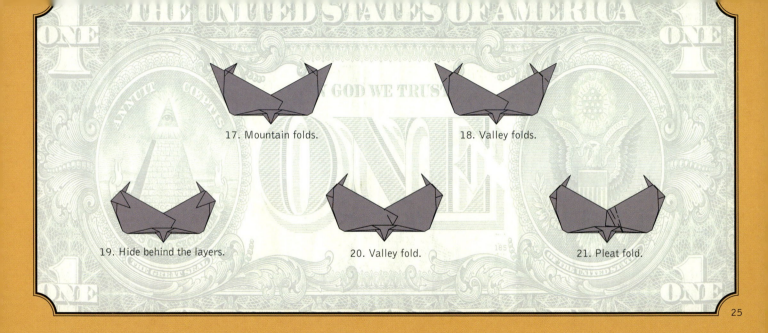

17. Mountain folds.

18. Valley folds.

19. Hide behind the layers.

20. Valley fold.

21. Pleat fold.

BATTLE STAR GALACTICA: RAIDER

22. Valley fold.

23. Pleat fold.

24. Pleat fold.

25. Pleat fold.

26. Turn over.

27. Valley folds.

28. Unfold the previous folds.

Completed Raider,
shown from the top.

DID YOU KNOW...

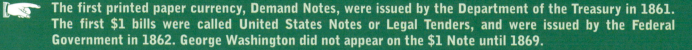

- The first printed paper currency, Demand Notes, were issued by the Department of the Treasury in 1861. The first $1 bills were called United States Notes or Legal Tenders, and were issued by the Federal Government in 1862. George Washington did not appear on the $1 Note until 1869.

- The Great Seal of the United States, which first appeared on the $1 Silver Certificate in 1935, was officially adopted by the United States in 1782. The seal still appears on the back of the $1 bill.

- The only people portrayed on currently circulating bills who were not presidents are Alexander Hamilton, the first Secretary of the Treasury, on the front of the $10 bill, and Benjamin Franklin, a statesman who signed the Declaration of Independence and helped frame the Constitution of the United States of America, on the front of the $100 bill.

⚹ BATTLE STAR GALACTICA: ANUBIS FIGHTER ⚹

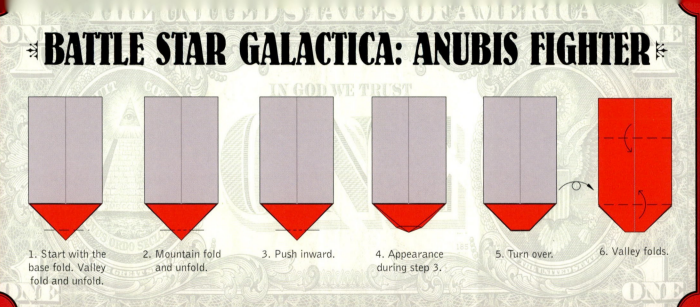

1. Start with the base fold. Valley fold and unfold.

2. Mountain fold and unfold.

3. Push inward.

4. Appearance during step 3.

5. Turn over.

6. Valley folds.

BATTLE STAR GALACTICA: ANUBIS FIGHTER

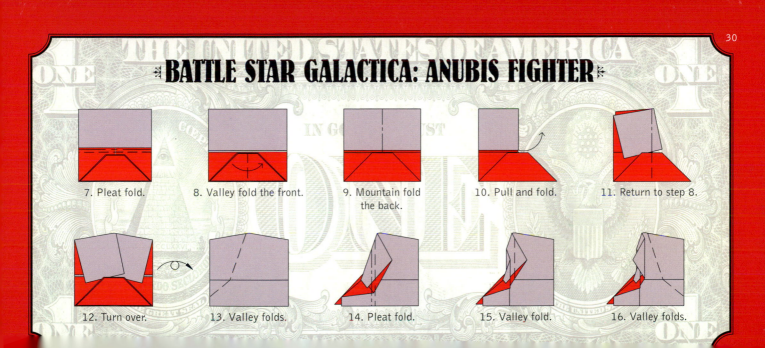

7. Pleat fold.

8. Valley fold the front.

9. Mountain fold the back.

10. Pull and fold.

11. Return to step 8.

12. Turn over.

13. Valley folds.

14. Pleat fold.

15. Valley fold.

16. Valley folds.

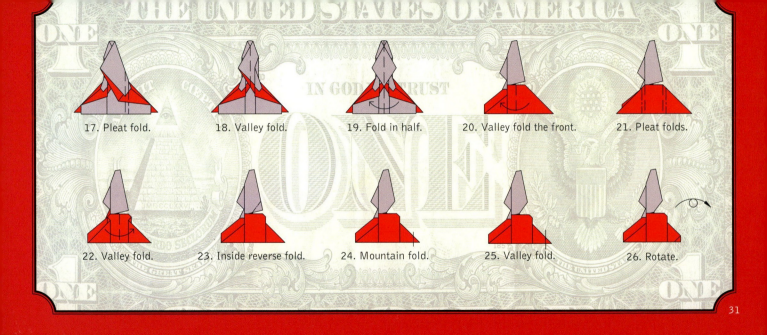

17. Pleat fold.

18. Valley fold.

19. Fold in half.

20. Valley fold the front.

21. Pleat folds.

22. Valley fold.

23. Inside reverse fold.

24. Mountain fold.

25. Valley fold.

26. Rotate.

✠ BATTLE STAR GALACTICA: ANUBIS FIGHTER ✠

27. Valley fold both the front and the back.

28. Mountain fold.

29. Valley fold.

30. Completed Anubis Fighter.

CONCORDE

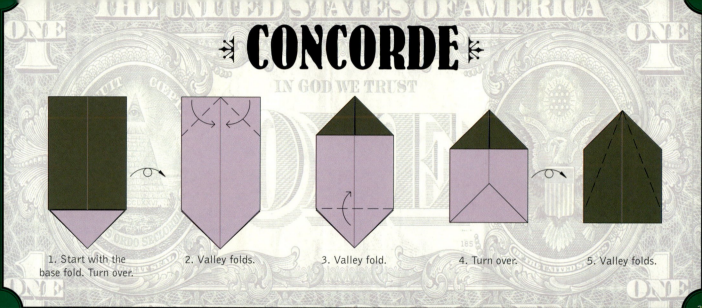

1. Start with the base fold. Turn over.

2. Valley folds.

3. Valley fold.

4. Turn over.

5. Valley folds.

❋ CONCORDE ❋

6. Turn over.

7. Valley folds.

8. Fold in half.

9. Valley fold and unfold both sides.

10. Valley folds.

11. Valley fold both sides.

12. Rotate.

13. Inside reverse fold.

14. Valley fold to level wings.

15. Mountain folds.

16. Valley folds.

17. Completed Concorde.

WORLD WAR II SINGLE ENGINE FIGHTER

— PART ONE —

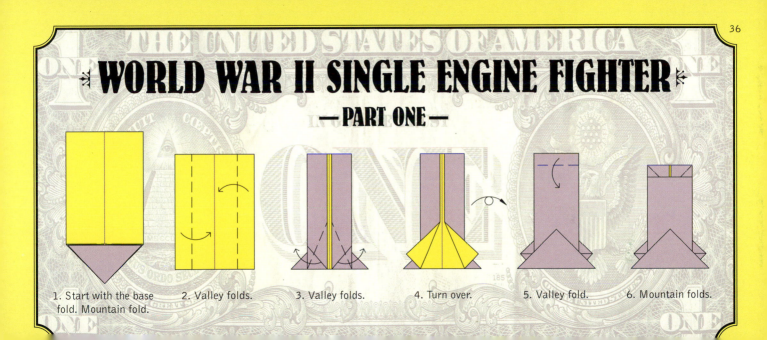

1. Start with the base fold. Mountain fold.

2. Valley folds.

3. Valley folds.

4. Turn over.

5. Valley fold.

6. Mountain folds.

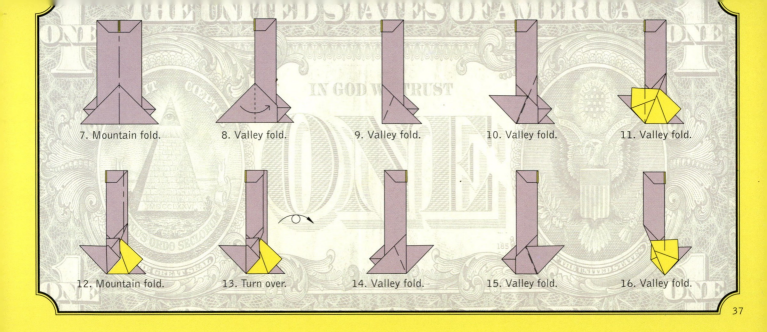

7. Mountain fold.

8. Valley fold.

9. Valley fold.

10. Valley fold.

11. Valley fold.

12. Mountain fold.

13. Turn over.

14. Valley fold.

15. Valley fold.

16. Valley fold.

WORLD WAR II SINGLE ENGINE FIGHTER

— PART ONE —

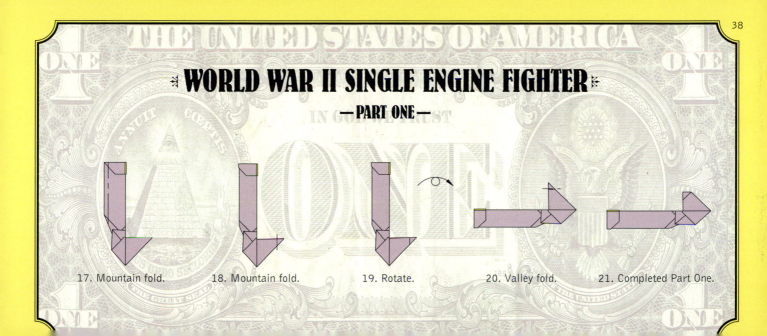

17. Mountain fold. 18. Mountain fold. 19. Rotate. 20. Valley fold. 21. Completed Part One.

— PART TWO —

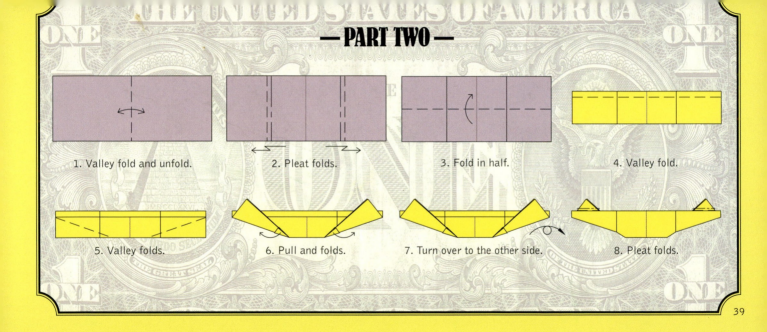

1. Valley fold and unfold.

2. Pleat folds.

3. Fold in half.

4. Valley fold.

5. Valley folds.

6. Pull and folds.

7. Turn over to the other side.

8. Pleat folds.

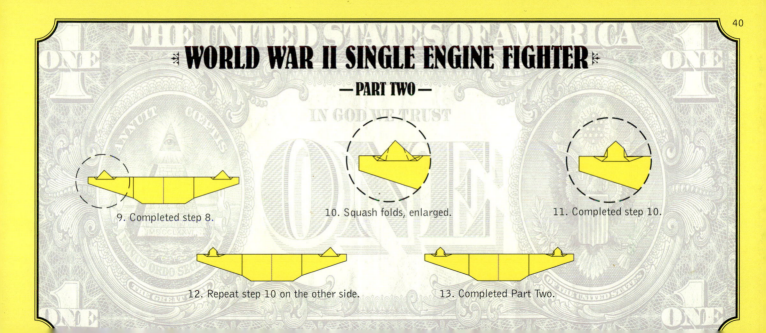

WORLD WAR II SINGLE ENGINE FIGHTER

— PART TWO —

9. Completed step 8.

10. Squash folds, enlarged.

11. Completed step 10.

12. Repeat step 10 on the other side.

13. Completed Part Two.

— ASSEMBLY —

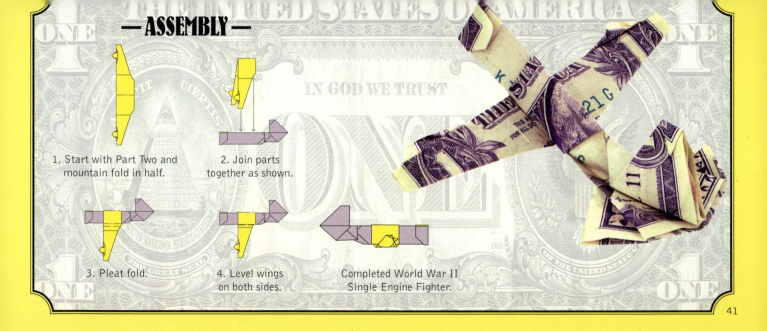

1. Start with Part Two and mountain fold in half.

2. Join parts together as shown.

3. Pleat fold.

4. Level wings on both sides.

Completed World War II Single Engine Fighter.

41

DID YOU KNOW...

"In God We Trust" was first printed on U.S. coins in 1864. In 1955, a law was passed requiring all money, paper and coins, to include the phrase in the design. It first appeared on the $1 Silver Certificate bill in 1957, and on all Federal Reserve Notes since 1963.

The faces appearing on the various dollar bills were chosen in 1929, and have not changed since. The Secretary of the Treasury is responsible for the selection of the designs and portraits.

The United States government introduced color in the $20 bill in 2003, done partly to make it harder to counterfeit. This is not the first time there has been color in our money; the $20 Gold Certificate, Series 1905 was tinted gold. Today, the new $20 and $50 still look like the traditional green money—the color is subtly in the background.

B-52 STRATOFORTRESS

— PART ONE —

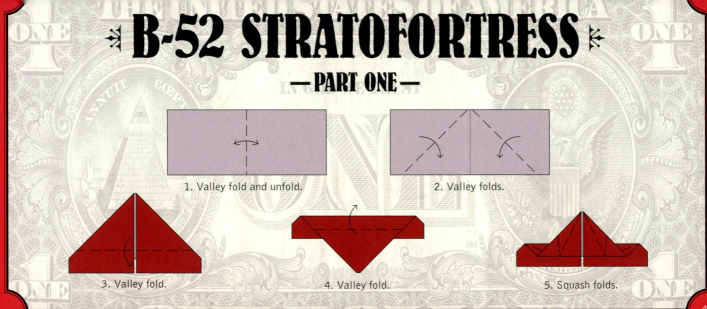

1. Valley fold and unfold.

2. Valley folds.

3. Valley fold.

4. Valley fold.

5. Squash folds.

B-52 STRATOFORTRESS

— PART ONE —

6. Appearance during step 5.

7. Valley folds.

8. Turn over to the other side.

9. Valley fold.

10. Valley fold and unfold.

11. Completed Part One.

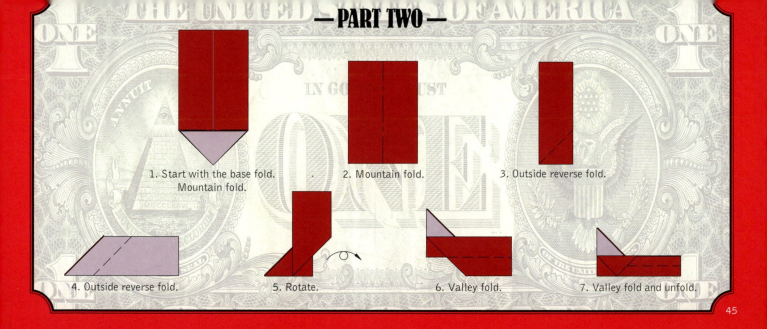

1. Start with the base fold. Mountain fold.

2. Mountain fold.

3. Outside reverse fold.

4. Outside reverse fold.

5. Rotate.

6. Valley fold.

7. Valley fold and unfold.

❈ B-52 STRATOFORTRESS ❈

— PART TWO —

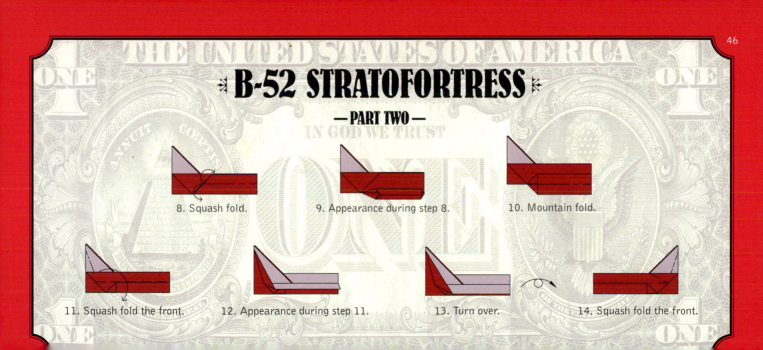

8. Squash fold.

9. Appearance during step 8.

10. Mountain fold.

11. Squash fold the front.

12. Appearance during step 11.

13. Turn over.

14. Squash fold the front.

15. Appearance during step 14.

16. Hide behind layer.

17. Pull down to level.

18. Turn over.

19. Hide behind layer.

20. Valley fold to level.

21. Completed Part Two.

185

47

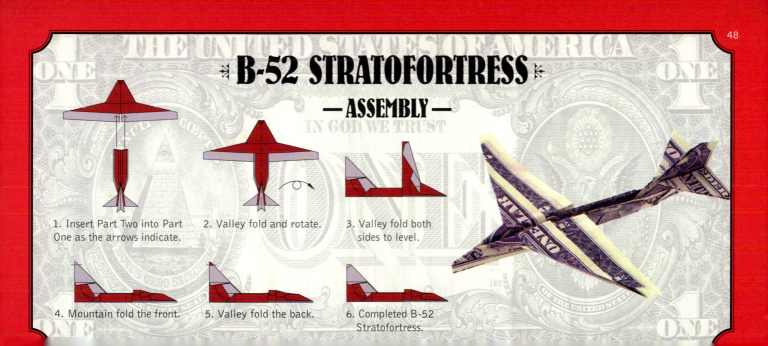

B-52 STRATOFORTRESS

— ASSEMBLY —

1. Insert Part Two into Part One as the arrows indicate.

2. Valley fold and rotate.

3. Valley fold both sides to level.

4. Mountain fold the front.

5. Valley fold the back.

6. Completed B-52 Stratofortress.

❊ F-15C EAGLE ❊

— PART ONE —

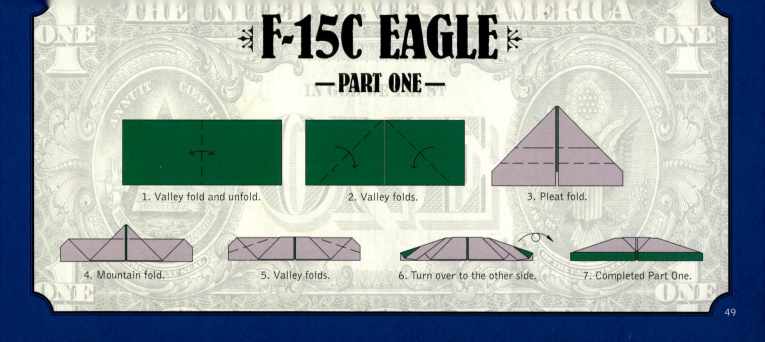

1. Valley fold and unfold.

2. Valley folds.

3. Pleat fold.

4. Mountain fold.

5. Valley folds.

6. Turn over to the other side.

7. Completed Part One.

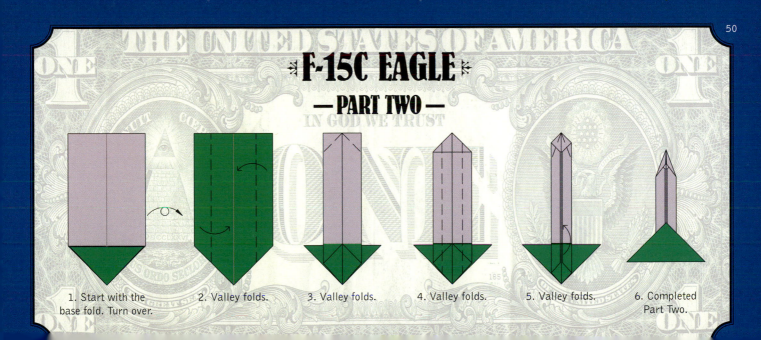

⚜ F-15C EAGLE ⚜
— PART TWO —

1. Start with the base fold. Turn over.

2. Valley folds.

3. Valley folds.

4. Valley folds.

5. Valley folds.

6. Completed Part Two.

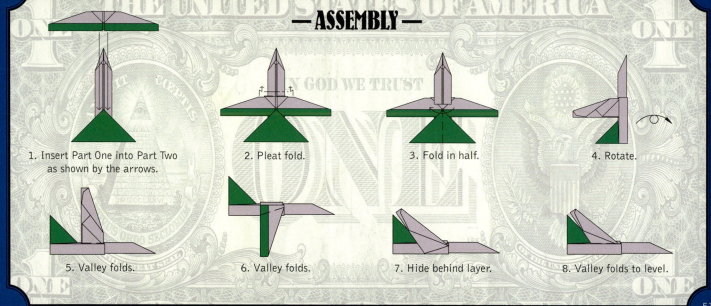

— ASSEMBLY —

1. Insert Part One into Part Two as shown by the arrows.

2. Pleat fold.

3. Fold in half.

4. Rotate.

5. Valley folds.

6. Valley folds.

7. Hide behind layer.

8. Valley folds to level.

❖ F-15C EAGLE ❖

— ASSEMBLY —

9. Pull to open the tails.

10. Completed
F-15C Eagle.

BOEING 747

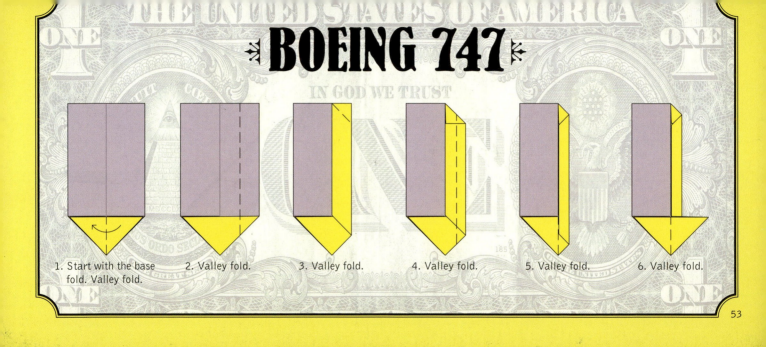

1. Start with the base fold. Valley fold.

2. Valley fold.

3. Valley fold.

4. Valley fold.

5. Valley fold.

6. Valley fold.

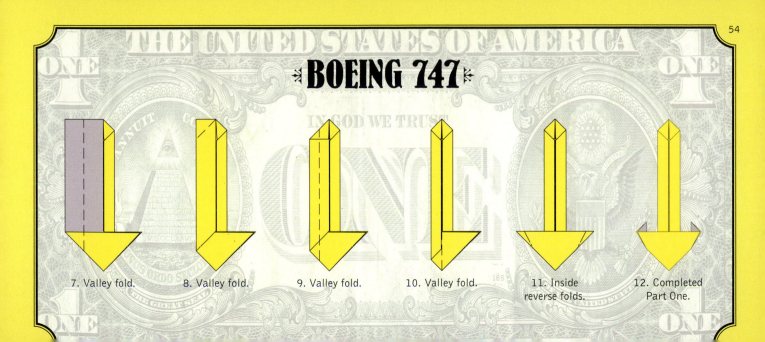

BOEING 747

7. Valley fold.

8. Valley fold.

9. Valley fold.

10. Valley fold.

11. Inside reverse folds.

12. Completed Part One.

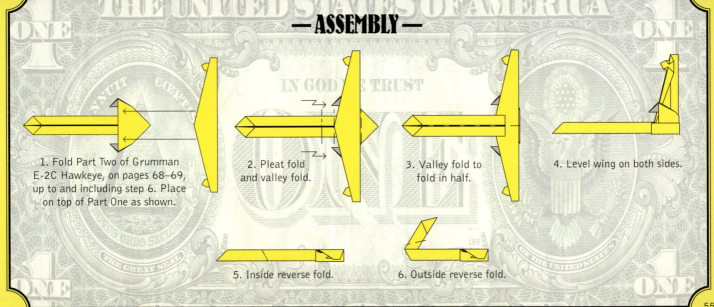

— ASSEMBLY —

1. Fold Part Two of Grumman E-2C Hawkeye, on pages 68–69, up to and including step 6. Place on top of Part One as shown.

2. Pleat fold and valley fold.

3. Valley fold to fold in half.

4. Level wing on both sides.

5. Inside reverse fold.

6. Outside reverse fold.

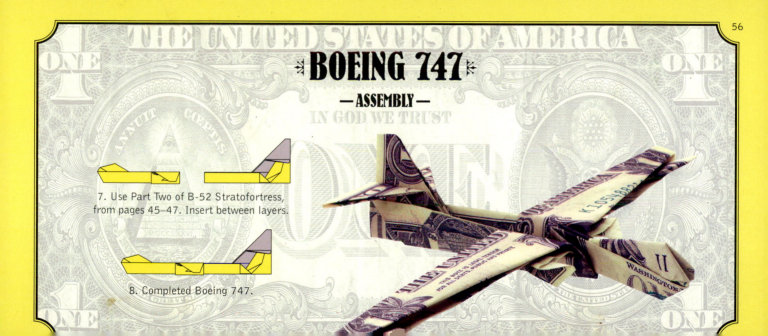

BOEING 747

— ASSEMBLY —

7. Use Part Two of B-52 Stratofortress, from pages 45–47. Insert between layers.

8. Completed Boeing 747.

DID YOU KNOW...

 The United States Treasury printed about 8.2 billion U.S. paper currency notes, at approximately 6 cents per note, during the Fiscal Year 2003.

 The most commonly used bill denominations in the United States today are the $1 bill and the $20 bill.

 Afraid of folding up your dollar bills? Don't worry, about 4,000 mountain and valley folds on the same fold line would be needed to tear the bill.

A-10A THUNDERBOLT

— PART ONE —

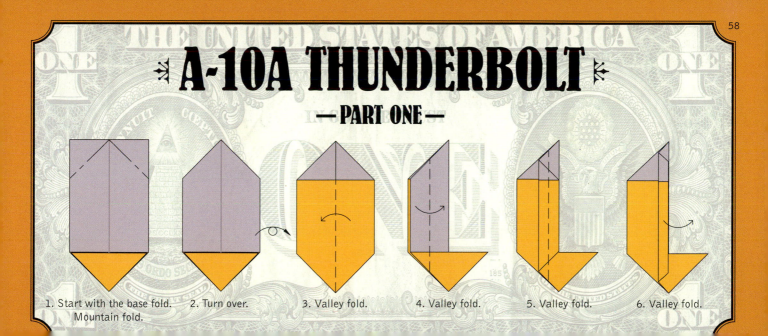

1. Start with the base fold. Mountain fold.

2. Turn over.

3. Valley fold.

4. Valley fold.

5. Valley fold.

6. Valley fold.

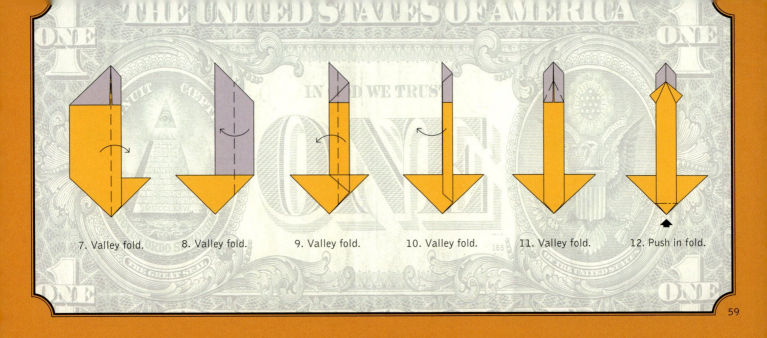

7. Valley fold. 8. Valley fold. 9. Valley fold. 10. Valley fold. 11. Valley fold. 12. Push in fold.

59

A-10A THUNDERBOLT

— PART ONE —

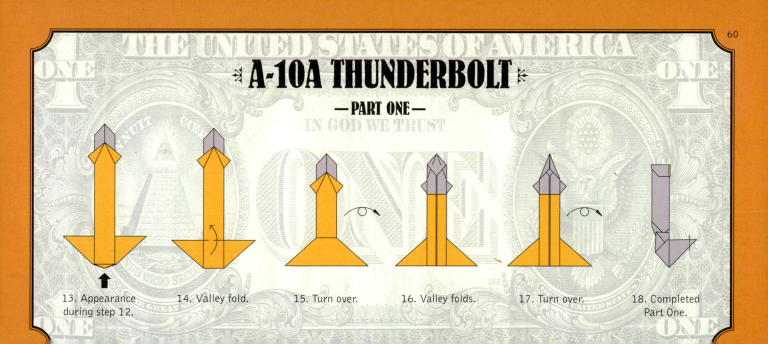

13. Appearance during step 12.

14. Valley fold.

15. Turn over.

16. Valley folds.

17. Turn over.

18. Completed Part One.

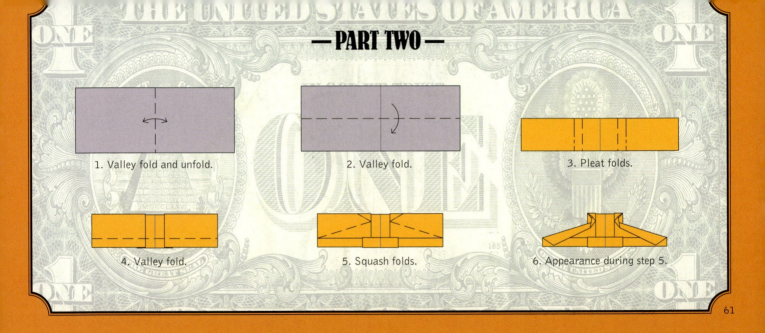

1. Valley fold and unfold.

2. Valley fold.

3. Pleat folds.

4. Valley fold.

5. Squash folds.

6. Appearance during step 5.

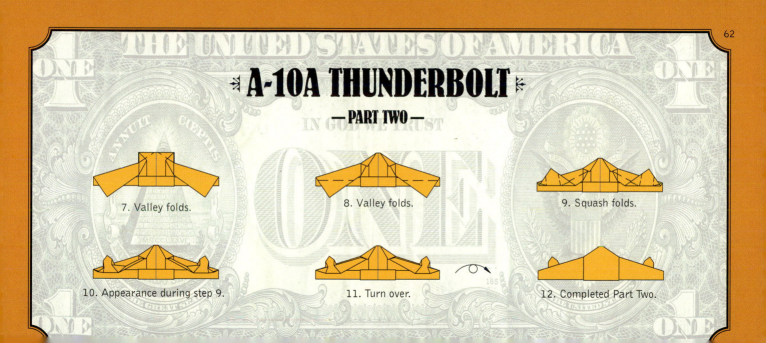

A-10A THUNDERBOLT

— PART TWO —

7. Valley folds.

8. Valley folds.

9. Squash folds.

10. Appearance during step 9.

11. Turn over.

12. Completed Part Two.

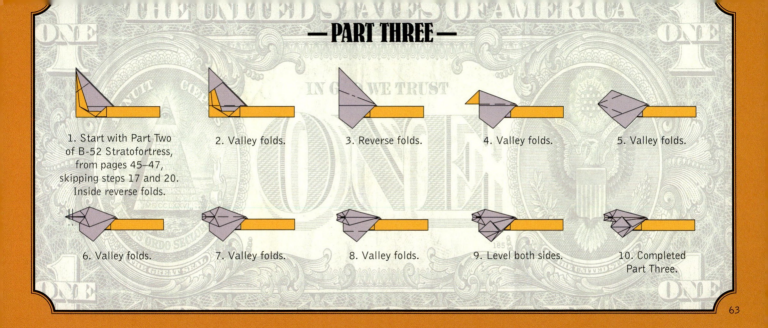

— PART THREE —

1. Start with Part Two of B-52 Stratofortress, from pages 45–47, skipping steps 17 and 20. Inside reverse folds.

2. Valley folds.

3. Reverse folds.

4. Valley folds.

5. Valley folds.

6. Valley folds.

7. Valley folds.

8. Valley folds.

9. Level both sides.

10. Completed Part Three.

A-10A THUNDERBOLT

— ASSEMBLY —

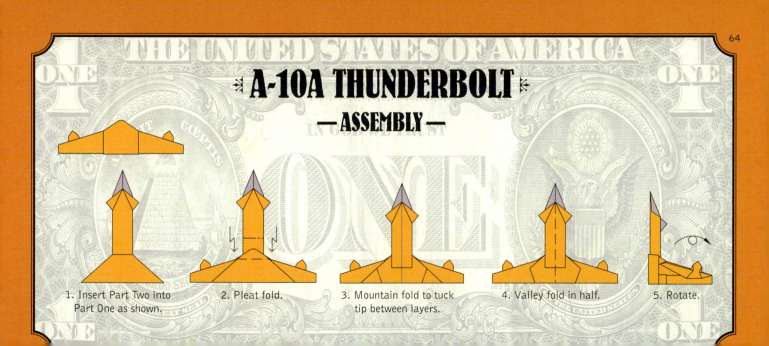

1. Insert Part Two into Part One as shown.

2. Pleat fold.

3. Mountain fold to tuck tip between layers.

4. Valley fold in half.

5. Rotate.

6. Mountain fold.   7. Valley fold to level wings.

8. Valley fold.   9. Completed step 8.

10. Insert Part Three between the wing layers.

11. Completed A-10A Thunderbolt.

GRUMMAN E-2C HAWKEYE

— PART ONE —

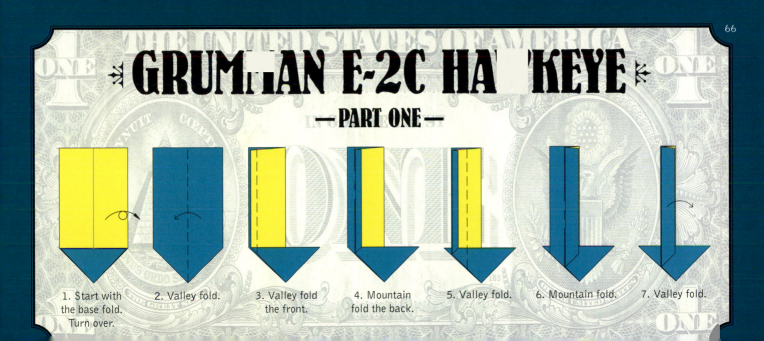

1. Start with the base fold. Turn over.

2. Valley fold.

3. Valley fold the front.

4. Mountain fold the back.

5. Valley fold.

6. Mountain fold.

7. Valley fold.

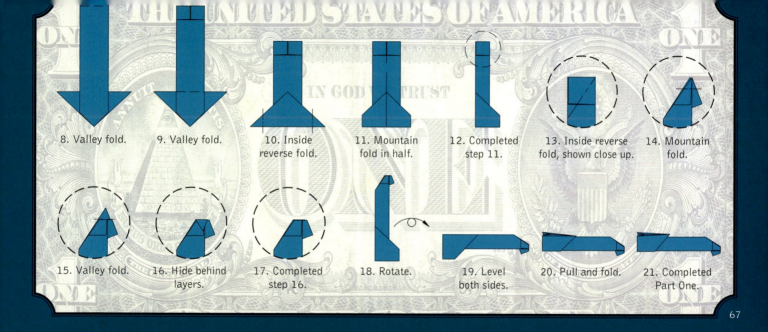

8. Valley fold.

9. Valley fold.

10. Inside reverse fold.

11. Mountain fold in half.

12. Completed step 11.

13. Inside reverse fold, shown close up.

14. Mountain fold.

15. Valley fold.

16. Hide behind layers.

17. Completed step 16.

18. Rotate.

19. Level both sides.

20. Pull and fold.

21. Completed Part One.

GRUMMAN E-2C HAWKEYE
— PART TWO —

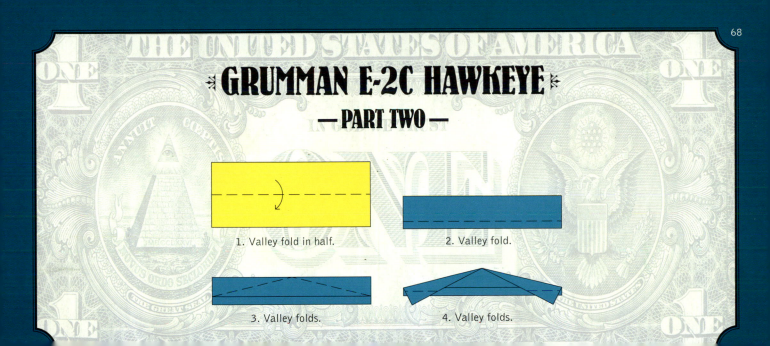

1. Valley fold in half.

2. Valley fold.

3. Valley folds.

4. Valley folds.

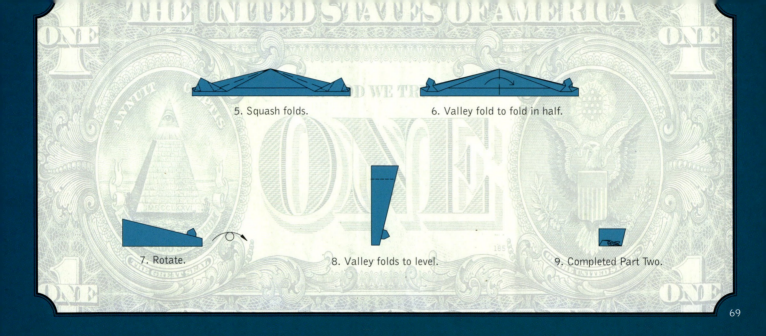

5. Squash folds.

6. Valley fold to fold in half.

7. Rotate.

8. Valley folds to level.

9. Completed Part Two.

GRUMMAN E-2C HAWKEYE
— PART THREE —

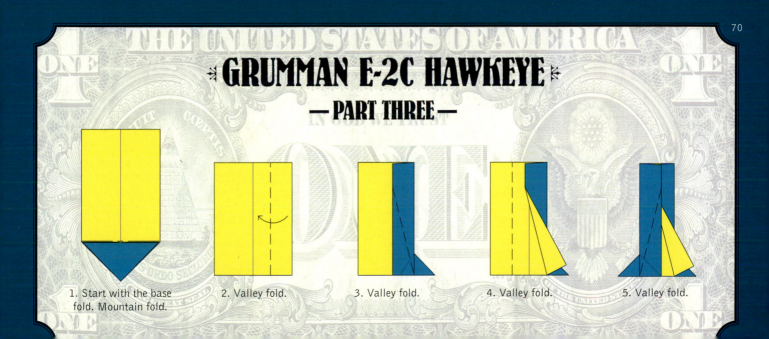

1. Start with the base fold. Mountain fold.

2. Valley fold.

3. Valley fold.

4. Valley fold.

5. Valley fold.

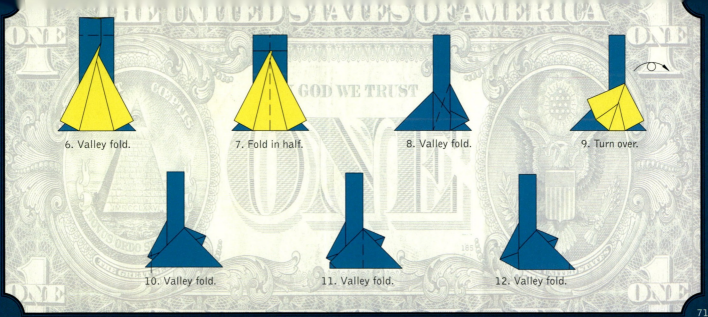

6. Valley fold.

7. Fold in half.

8. Valley fold.

9. Turn over.

10. Valley fold.

11. Valley fold.

12. Valley fold.

❅ GRUMMAN E-2C HAWKEYE ❅

— PART THREE —

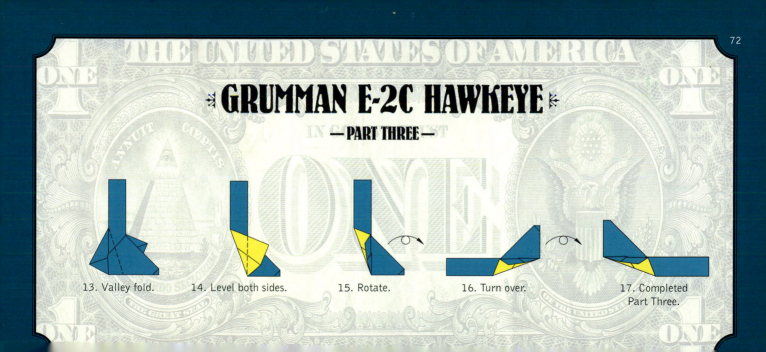

13. Valley fold.

14. Level both sides.

15. Rotate.

16. Turn over.

17. Completed Part Three.

1. Insert Part Three between layers of Part One as shown.

2. Insert Part Two in between layers of Part One, as shown.

3. Completed Grumman E-2C Hawkeye.

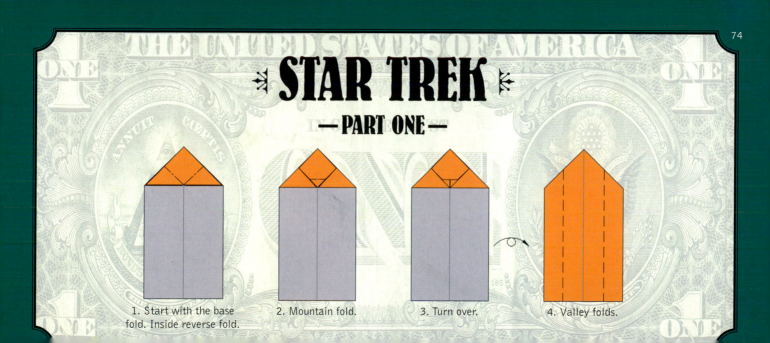

STAR TREK

— PART ONE —

1. Start with the base fold. Inside reverse fold.

2. Mountain fold.

3. Turn over.

4. Valley folds.

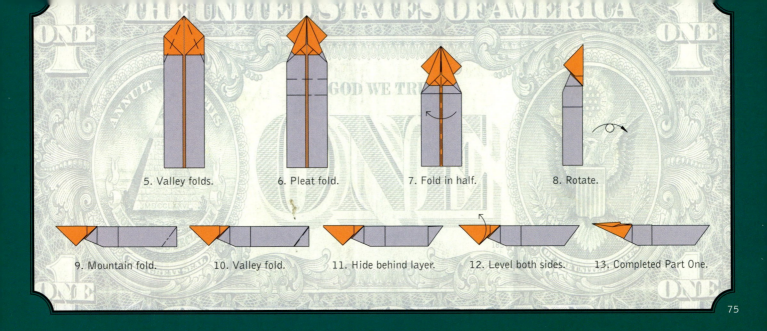

5. Valley folds.

6. Pleat fold.

7. Fold in half.

8. Rotate.

9. Mountain fold.

10. Valley fold.

11. Hide behind layer.

12. Level both sides.

13. Completed Part One.

❊ STAR TREK ❊

— PART TWO —

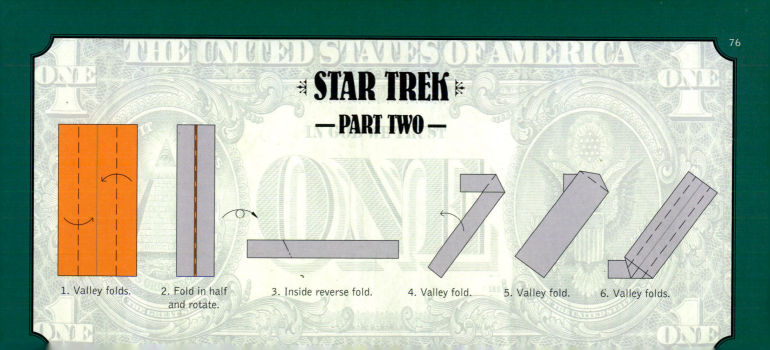

1. Valley folds.

2. Fold in half and rotate.

3. Inside reverse fold.

4. Valley fold.

5. Valley fold.

6. Valley folds.

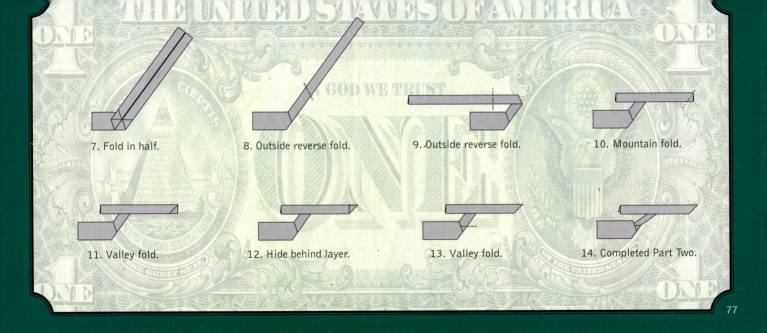

7. Fold in half.

8. Outside reverse fold.

9. Outside reverse fold.

10. Mountain fold.

11. Valley fold.

12. Hide behind layer.

13. Valley fold.

14. Completed Part Two.

✳ STAR TREK ✳
— PART THREE —

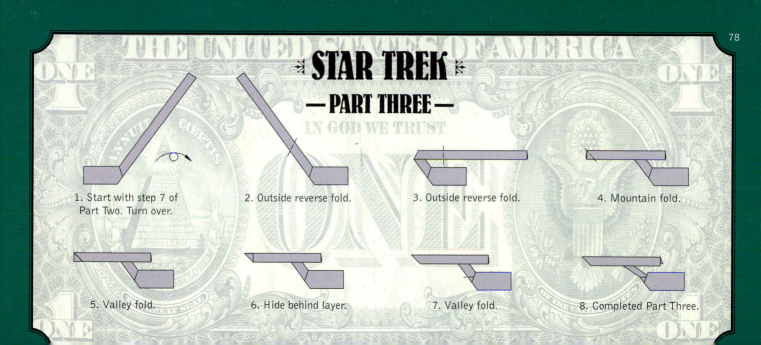

1. Start with step 7 of Part Two. Turn over.

2. Outside reverse fold.

3. Outside reverse fold.

4. Mountain fold.

5. Valley fold.

6. Hide behind layer.

7. Valley fold.

8. Completed Part Three.

1. Insert Part Two and Part Three into the openings between the layers of Part One.

2. Valley fold both sides.

3. Completed Star Trek.

INDEX